DAISY
and the
DIRTY DOZEN

Written & Illustrated by
BRIAN WALLACE

Edited by
JESSICA WALLACE

For Cole & Claire

Daisy and the Dirty Dozen
Written and Illustrated by Brian Wallace
Published by Newport Press

All rights reserved. No part of this book may be reproduced or transmitted in any form or by any means, electronic or mechanical, including photocopying, recording, or by an information storage and retrieval system - except by a reviewer who may quote brief passages in a review to be printed in a magazine or newspaper - without permission in writing from the publisher.

Copyright © 2018 by Brian Wallace

ISBN 978-0-692-08971-2 (Perfect Bound, Softcover)
ISBN 978-0-692-09139-5 (Case Laminate, Hardcover)
ISBN 978-0-692-09364-1 (eBook)

See the real life Daisy and the Dirty Dozen at www.daisyandthedirtydozen.com

One morning, Mr. Wallace stepped to the kitchen window. He looked out and saw something quite peculiar. A female mallard duck was swimming in the family pool.

Although it didn't happen often, this wasn't the first time a duck had come to swim at the Wallaces. In fact, this was the third or fourth time he had seen a mallard in the pool.

One time, he even saw both a hen and a drake stop by for a quick swim. (A female duck is called a *hen* and a male duck is called a *drake*.)

The Wallaces continued to see the duck over the next few weeks. By then, they suspected it was the same one each time. She would typically come for a morning swim and leave after a few minutes. The duck began visiting so often, Mr. Wallace gave her a name. He started calling her Daisy.

The Wallace family didn't see Daisy every morning, but they would sometimes find a puddle at the edge of the pool. It was a sign that Daisy had paid a visit. She always got out of the pool in the same spot.

Late one night, Mr. and Mrs. Wallace were awakened by a loud quacking. They had never heard such a thing in the middle of the night. Mr. Wallace rushed downstairs and turned on the lights. He found Daisy in the pool. The quacking was so loud and persistent. He began waving his arms and making noise to scare Daisy away. After a few minutes, she flew off.

Mr. Wallace knew very little about ducks, and although he did enjoy seeing Daisy stop by for her morning swim, he wasn't too enthusiastic about a duck waking up the entire neighborhood in the middle of the night. So he began reading about ducks and what to expect if one decided to move into your backyard.

What he discovered was quite unsettling. He read that if a duck swam in your pool, the pool would be ruined forever. He read about the mess a duck would make. He read that if ducks made your pool their home, they would return each year.

And lastly, he read that if a duck laid eggs in your yard, the family would stay until they all learned to fly. It takes ducks about two months before they are able to fly!

That night, after he finished his duck research, Mr. Wallace decided that he wasn't prepared to deal with a duck moving in, or even worse, a whole family of ducks living in the family swimming pool. So, he filled the pool with pool toys, kayaks and anything else he could find that would float. He had read that ducks wouldn't land in the pool if there were objects floating in it. They would scare the ducks away.

The next morning, he learned that what he read was not true.

Once they realized they couldn't scare her away, the Wallaces began to think something else might be going on. They stepped behind the pool gate and quietly watched Daisy. She disappeared into a bush near the pool. Mr. Wallace realized she may have laid her nest in the bushes. Their pool toys and shoo tactics were too late.

Mr. Wallace told Cole and Claire that the family would have to give Daisy her space now and that they needed to be respectful of Daisy's soon-to-be growing family. They started talking about what an honor it was that Daisy chose their yard for her babies' first home.

The next day, Daisy was back, of course. Mr. Wallace was certain that he heard peeps coming from the bush, but he didn't dare go in for a closer look. He was finished being scary.

Late the next afternoon, the family dog, Henry, went out to the backyard to do what dogs do. To his surprise, there were visitors in the side yard—Daisy and her 12 ducklings! When they saw Henry, Daisy and the ducklings rushed to safety by running under the gate and jumping into the pool.

Mrs. Wallace immediately called Mr. Wallace. "We have 12 ducklings in the pool! They're here! What should I do? Will they know how to swim already? What if they can't get out of the pool?!" she exclaimed.

Mr. Wallace had expected this day would come. He was already on his way to pick up a board at the local hardware store so he could build them a ramp. He knew the ducklings would be too small to climb out of the pool and the ramp would give them a way to walk out.

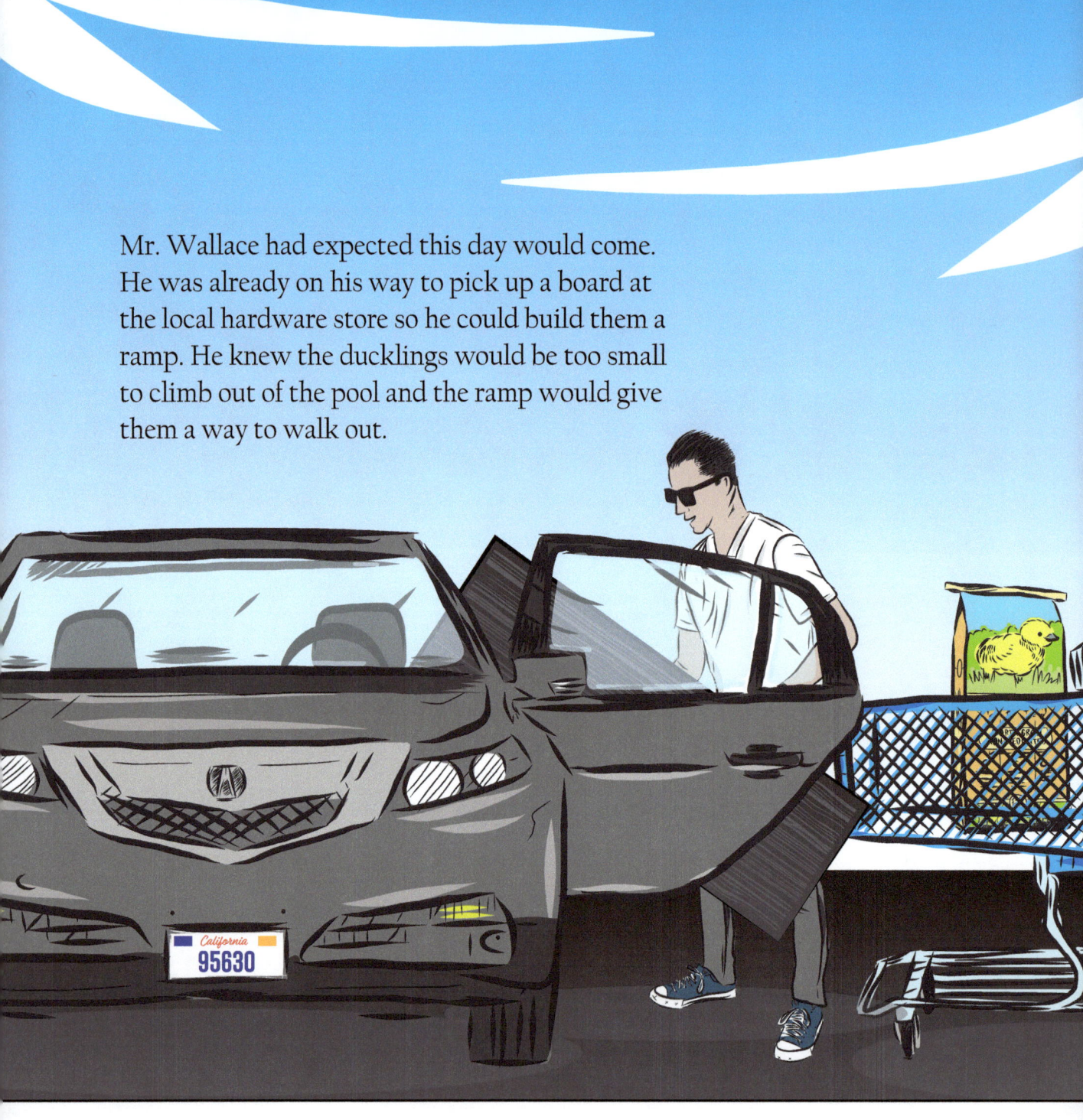

Mr. Wallace also made a stop at the feed store. He bought food for the ducklings because he didn't think they could survive on what they found in the yard. These babies were going to grow up healthy and safe!

Soon after they discovered the ducklings, Cole found the nest with the broken egg shells. Daisy had been sitting in these bushes for almost a month and the Wallaces had no idea!

Mr. and Mrs. Wallace put the ramp in place and set out a tray for the ducklings' food. They quickly figured out how to use the ramp and they loved the food, but soon it was all over the yard and in the pool.

Daisy was always mindful to drop food in the pool for the ducklings that continued swimming while the other ducklings ate. Within just a few days, the pool area was littered with the ducklings' food.

It didn't matter though; the Wallace family was in love.

For the first few nights, the ducklings slept huddled together in a pile under Daisy's protective wings. They quickly outgrew her wings, but continued to sleep together under Daisy's ever-watchful eye.

The ducklings were identical and impossible to tell apart. Cole and Claire wanted to name them, but they all looked exactly the same. Mr. Wallace started calling them the Dirty Dozen. Every day he went out and tried to tidy up the pool area, but the ducklings were very messy (as he had read).

Each day, the ducklings grew bigger.
Daisy was teaching them how to survive in the wild.

She taught them how to stay very still.
She taught them how to dive to the bottom of the pool.
She taught them how to find bugs to eat.

After a few days, the ducklings didn't really even need the ramp. They figured out how to climb up the step and could get in and out of the pool without help.

Even though the ducklings were getting bigger, they watched their mama and stayed close to her. They would swim right beside her, and sometimes ride on her back! All 12 ducklings were never out of Daisy's sight.

The Wallace family was enjoying their visitors. Each time Mrs. Wallace walked by the kitchen window she would quickly count the ducklings to make sure they were all still there. Mr. and Mrs. Wallace would sip their morning coffee by the pool so they could watch the ducks. It was better than any TV show! Claire would sing and play her ukulele for her feathered friends. Even though the Wallaces never touched the ducks, it felt good to be part of their first family.

Daisy and her ducklings would spend the day exploring the yard (but they went back to Henry's side very cautiously). All 13 ducks would swim in the pool and march through the flower beds. Mr. Wallace was sure they were going to stay until the ducklings could fly.

The ducks loved the Wallace backyard. One day, Mrs. Wallace saw Daisy and all of her ducklings climb to the top of the pool slide and slide right into the water. It was amazing—and amusing! They felt at home in the Wallace backyard.

When the ducklings were about one week old, the Wallaces woke up to the ducklings swimming alone in the pool. The Wallaces and the ducklings were worried and confused. Where was Daisy?

Moments later, Daisy flew in and landed in the pool with a splash! The ducklings rushed to her side and Mr. and Mrs. Wallace breathed a sigh of relief. They knew they couldn't take care of and teach the ducklings nearly as well as Daisy could.

Many friends and neighbors were excited to hear about this family of ducks living nearby and they came over to the Wallace house to see for themselves. One night, there was a big party in the neighborhood and a crowd of people came over to the Wallace's yard to see Daisy and the Dirty Dozen. Everyone was so excited to see them with their own eyes, but the ducks were not used to this kind of noise and attention!

One afternoon, Mr. Wallace came home, looked out the window, and discovered that Daisy and the ducklings were nowhere to be found. He knew this day would come, but he didn't expect it so soon. He had grown attached to those ducks. He loved seeing them every morning. Just weeks before, he had filled his pool full of brightly colored toys hoping to keep Daisy away, and now he knew that he was going to miss them all. The pool seemed too empty and still.

A little later that day, there was a knock at the front door. A neighbor told Mr. Wallace that Daisy and her ducklings had walked across the street and spent the afternoon in her yard. They were on the move... probably making their way to the pond nearby. After a few hours at the neighbor's house, they had vanished again. The Wallaces worried a bit because the ducklings didn't fly yet, but felt better when they thought about how well Daisy took care of them in the two weeks they lived in the backyard.

Nobody is quite sure where Daisy and the Dirty Dozen were headed, but there are many creeks and ponds nearby that would make a perfect home. The ducks likely waddled to one of those.

Even now, whenever the Wallaces see a mallard, they wonder if it could be one of the babies all grown up now – or even Daisy herself. They will always remember their duck family with love.

www.ingramcontent.com/pod-product-compliance
Lightning Source LLC
Chambersburg PA
CBHW042147290426
44110CB00003B/143